This book belongs to:

..........................................................................................................................

# FANTASTIC DRAGONS
## And How To Draw Them

## Tom Kidd

Search Press

A QUARTO BOOK

This edition published in 2018 by
Search Press Ltd
Wellwood
North Farm Road
Tunbridge Wells
Kent TN2 3DR
United Kingdom

Copyright © 2018 Quarto Publishing plc
An imprint of The Quarto Group

ISBN 978-1-78221-680-3

Conceived, edited and designed by
Quarto Publishing plc
The Old Brewery
6 Blundell Street
London N7 9BH

www.quartoknows.com

QUAR.FDAH

Editor: Claire Waite Brown
Designer: Hugh Schermuly
Art director: Caroline Guest
Publisher: Samantha Warrington

Printed in China

# CONTENTS

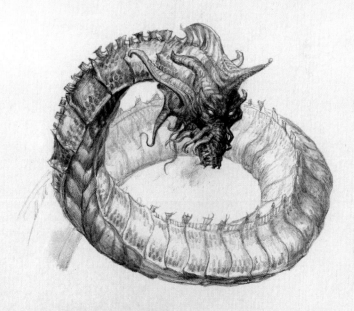

# FOREWORD

The dragon is certainly a mythical
creature. There are no dragons on
Earth, but my intention with this book
is to teach you how to draw them in a
way that they seem to live and
breathe – fire.

The greatest fun you can have with art
is making things up using your
imagination. It seems like an easy
task, but doing it well is actually more
difficult than copying something.
Think about it – a test would be a
whole lot easier if you were allowed to
refer to a textbook when you took it.

To help you get to grips with the
difficult process of drawing from your
imagination, this interactive workbook
goes one better than a textbook, and
features exercises, examples
and techniques that you can copy
and practise.

Once you've built yourself a visual library, you can start inventing your own creatures. My job here is to teach you a structure you can build on infinitely. The basics of creating dragons are the basics for inventing any creature and, more generally, for any kind of imaginative art.

The world we live in today is filled with visual information, and using the Internet you can quickly find a picture of just about anything on the planet and within the solar system. However, taking a picture doesn't give you an understanding of something. The only way to understand something well is to draw it. There are literal and physical levels of understanding. To create dragons, you'll need to explore all levels.

# DRAGON ANATOMY

A dragon is much more than the sum of its parts; however, studying those parts separately will help you understand how dragons are structured.

This section breaks down the dragon's anatomy into its basic parts, and by doing so will furnish you with your tools for invention.

There is a wide range of creatures that fall into the dragon category. Clearly they can't all be members of the same species; the variances between them are too great. Mythology pays little attention to science, but fantasy artists are entrusted with making mythological creatures plausible, and you will find this section integral to that purpose.

# HEAD AND FACE

In general, a dragon's head can look like that of a lizard, a horse or even a lion. Combining various forms will make your dragon more dangerous or more regal. Allow your mind to meld the references together in a pleasing, natural manner.

*This dragon's penetrating gaze has all the intensity of a vulture stare.*

**Inspiration from nature**
Spend time studying the vast variety of head shapes in the animal kingdom. Note where the jaw hinges appear and the array of expressions revealed by different creatures.

*Fig. 1:* Vulture
*Fig. 2:* Frilled lizard displaying
*Fig. 3:* Iguana
*Fig. 4:* Fish skeleton
*Fig. 5:* Head of a seahorse
*Fig. 6:* Crocodile
*Fig. 7:* Saw viper

Use these pages to collect your own examples of heads and faces from nature, reference books and the Internet. Make notes to help you recall what it is that drew you to particular images, and how you might use this in your own dragon art.

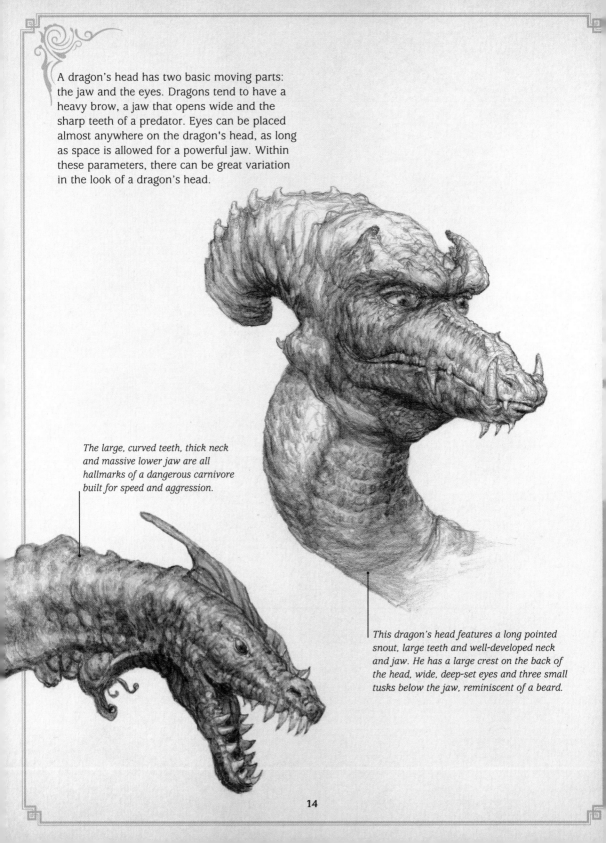

A dragon's head has two basic moving parts: the jaw and the eyes. Dragons tend to have a heavy brow, a jaw that opens wide and the sharp teeth of a predator. Eyes can be placed almost anywhere on the dragon's head, as long as space is allowed for a powerful jaw. Within these parameters, there can be great variation in the look of a dragon's head.

*The large, curved teeth, thick neck and massive lower jaw are all hallmarks of a dangerous carnivore built for speed and aggression.*

*This dragon's head features a long pointed snout, large teeth and well-developed neck and jaw. He has a large crest on the back of the head, wide, deep-set eyes and three small tusks below the jaw, reminiscent of a beard.*

Copy the examples here, or have a go at your own dragon heads. Imagine the skull as a solid structure composed of a series of planes.

## Expression

A dragon's personality manifests itself in its face, so you should give your dragons expressive faces. There is a wealth of personality traits that can be applied. In literature you will find many stories about very clever dragons. If you're making a sentient dragon, its face must show intelligence. The best way to do this is to give the dragon a humanlike expression; for example, by including a raised eyebrow, a kind smile or a thoughtful gesture. Similarly, an aggressive dragon will need to show its fangs.

*This dragon has a gentle, friendly expression.*

*A benign and intelligent-looking creature, this dragon is nearly smiling.*

*This short-snouted beast with exposed teeth, exaggerated brows and jutting head appears threatening. Here, body language conveys more about the dragon's nature and intent than any individual feature.*

Here's your chance to experiment with dragon facial expressions. What characteristics can you convey through the face alone?

Continue your exploration of dragon heads and faces here.

# EYES

A dragon's eyes can range from small to large, from insect to reptile to mammal, and may appear anywhere on the dragon's skull. It's not even required that a dragon has two eyes; you can make it have as many as you want. The only real requirement is that the dragon has to look like a dragon.

**Inspiration from nature**
With thorough research, you'll hit upon the right eye shape and eye colour for your dragon.

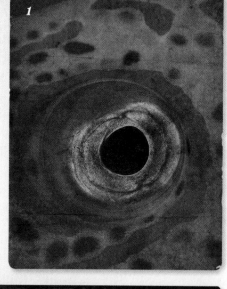

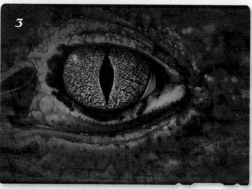

*Your dragon can take on the characteristics of different animals. This dragon resembles an alligator, but his big eyes and heavy lids make him seem devilishly clever like a fox.*

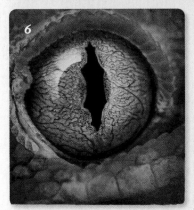

*Fig. 1:* Fish
*Fig. 2:* Cat
*Fig. 3:* Crocodile
*Fig. 4:* Frog
*Fig. 5:* Eagle
*Fig. 6:* Gecko
*Fig. 7:* Jumping spider
*Fig. 8:* Iguana

Look for your own examples of eyes in the natural world and attach or sketch them out on these pages. Make a note of what you like about each image and consider how you might translate these characteristics to your own dragons.

An animal that is a hunter tends to have eyes that face forwards for the sake of binocular vision. With dragons, however, this is not a solid rule, so you can place your dragon's eyes where you feel they look best. It's standard practice to put the dragon's eyes on the sides of the skull, but you can place them in between the front and the sides.

To place a dragon in a specific environment, you need to have a plausible explanation for the form and for its purpose. A good example of interesting eye placement is that of the crocodile. Its eyes are positioned on top of its head because it lurks beneath the water waiting for its prey to come near.

## Behind the eyes

Eyes are crucial to facial expression, and your dragon's eyes should say something about it. Is it friend or foe? Open, rounded eyes are relaxed and passive. Eyebrows brought together shade the eyes from glare and indicate cunningness or thought, while arched eyebrows and upper lids indicate aggression. The eyes will lead the head and indicate feelings more clearly than anything else on the face, so it's important to study the muscles and structure around the eye and understand how they change in appearance based on what your dragon is feeling.

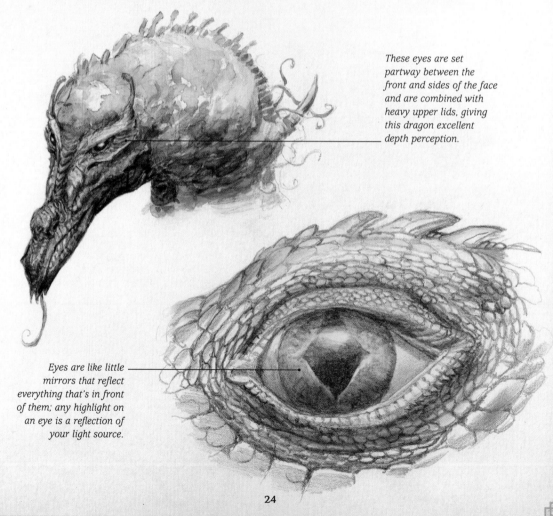

*These eyes are set partway between the front and sides of the face and are combined with heavy upper lids, giving this dragon excellent depth perception.*

*Eyes are like little mirrors that reflect everything that's in front of them; any highlight on an eye is a reflection of your light source.*

Experiment with eye shape and structure to discover the many expressions they can describe.

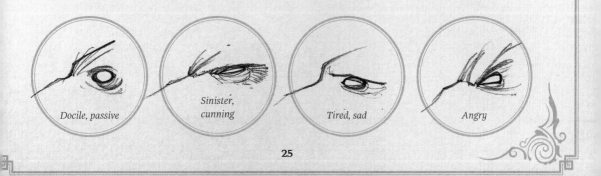

Docile, passive

Sinister, cunning

Tired, sad

Angry

You can use these pages to experiment with eye shape, placement and expression.

# WINGS

A dragon's wings are made of bone and skin and are similar to bat wings. A dragon can wrap itself in its wings or close them tightly at its sides. Of course, you are not held to the bat form for the dragon wing, but it's worth studying closely.

**Inspiration from nature**
Wings take many different forms and work in different ways. Study bird wings, bat wings or even lizard wings.

*The dragon's inner wing is lit from above and shows the wing structure in silhouette. Note how the translucency of the wings illustrates their hand-like qualities.*

*Fig. 1:* Bat at rest
*Fig. 2:* Eagle soaring
*Fig. 3:* Heron landing
*Fig. 4:* Flying lizard
*Fig. 5:* Bat flying

Collect your own wing examples here. Record how the wings work and how they are used by their owner, to refer back to when creating your own flying dragons.

The skin is stretched out tight between the 'fingers' of the dragon wing, much like the fabric of an umbrella when it's opened. In both the dragon and the bat, the small muscles in the wing can control it much better than the locked stretchers of an umbrella do.

Because the skin is stretched thin on a dragon wing, it is translucent. In many cases you can see the light coming through, silhouetting the wing bones. This is something you should, of course, consider carefully when drawing your dragon's wings.

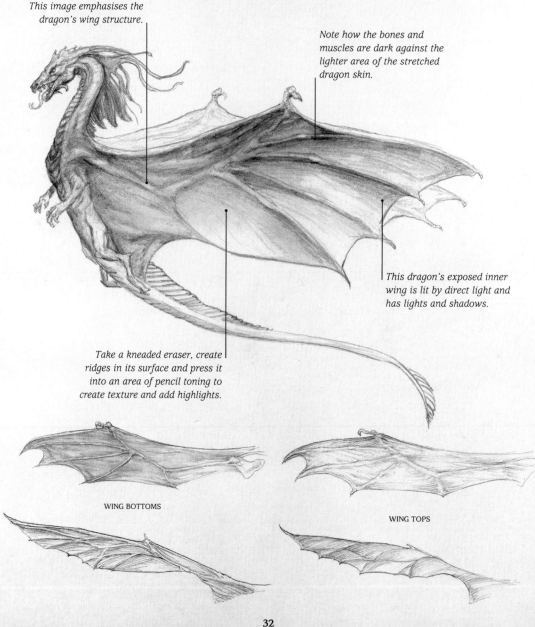

*This image emphasises the dragon's wing structure.*

*Note how the bones and muscles are dark against the lighter area of the stretched dragon skin.*

*This dragon's exposed inner wing is lit by direct light and has lights and shadows.*

*Take a kneaded eraser, create ridges in its surface and press it into an area of pencil toning to create texture and add highlights.*

WING BOTTOMS

WING TOPS

Copy the drawings opposite to help you get to grips with wing structure.

### Wing movement

This sequence illustrates some standard wing positions for forwards flight. Note that the dragon's head lifts up and down and that its arms move a little; however, the dragon will be most aerodynamic if it tucks in its arms, as you can see when the dragon's wings are up.

**Practice making your dragon fly by copying these wing positions.**

### In flight

To fly efficiently, a dragon will need to form its body into an aerodynamic shape. The better it can flatten its arms and legs to its body, the better it will fly.

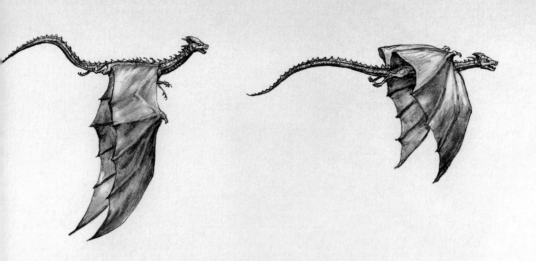

## Multiuse wings

Unlike birds, both bats and dragons can use their wings for things other than flying. Bats use the 'thumbs' of their wings for grasping, and so do dragons. Depending on the type of dragon, they'll use their wings differently. If your dragon has two legs and two wings, it will likely have to use its wings for walking, the same way a bat does. The dragon will move the same way you'd expect a four-legged animal to move about but will be a bit awkward. A six-limbed dragon will walk on its four legs and keep its wings tucked in as it proceeds, leaving them free for use in battle. The thumbs will then become weapons similar to an ice pick. Because a dragon's wings have a very long reach, with the longest bones in a dragon's body, this will be a deadly weapon indeed – only second to its ability to breathe fire.

### Wing details

At times, you'll want to have your dragons in activities with their wings pulled in, so you'll need to know how the skeleton of the wing compresses. To aid you in your understanding, study the human hand, since its structure is similar to that of the dragon wing.

1 Thumbs
2 Fingers
3 Palms
4 Knuckles
5 Wrist bones
6 Skin between fingers
7 Scapula
8 Elbow

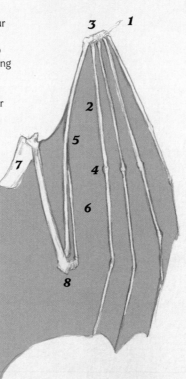

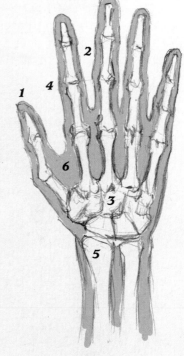

### Protective pose

A dragon can fold its wings around itself to create a pocket of warmth or to protect its face from wind and sandstorms. In this case, the dragon is using its wings to block the glare of the sun from its eyes.

Try drawing different functions for your dragon's wings.

Use these two pages to draw different types of wings, their anatomy and their use.

# NECKS AND TAILS

Although the simplest parts of the dragon, the long neck can propel the dragon's head forwards to take a terrible bite or swell to spit fire, while the tail, full of fierce movement and grace, reveals the dragon's feelings and illustrates its actions.

**Inspiration from nature**
There are a range of creatures from the land and sea to inspire you. Pay close attention to the curves and lines of each, and use these as the base from which to build your dragon's neck and tail.

Fig. 1: Aggressive swan
Fig. 2: Heron
Fig. 3: Snake
Fig. 4: Giraffe
Fig. 5: Coiled chameleon tail
Fig. 6: Scorpion
Fig. 7: Lobster tail
Fig. 8: Cactus

Use these pages to collect your own examples of necks and tails from nature, reference books and the Internet. Make notes to help you recall what it is that drew you to particular images, and how you might use this in your own dragon art.

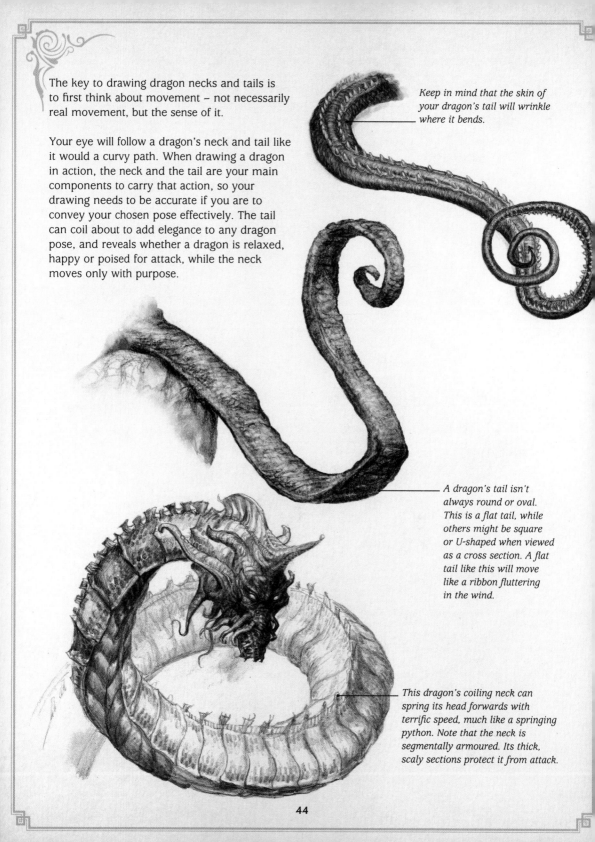

The key to drawing dragon necks and tails is to first think about movement – not necessarily real movement, but the sense of it.

Your eye will follow a dragon's neck and tail like it would a curvy path. When drawing a dragon in action, the neck and the tail are your main components to carry that action, so your drawing needs to be accurate if you are to convey your chosen pose effectively. The tail can coil about to add elegance to any dragon pose, and reveals whether a dragon is relaxed, happy or poised for attack, while the neck moves only with purpose.

*Keep in mind that the skin of your dragon's tail will wrinkle where it bends.*

*A dragon's tail isn't always round or oval. This is a flat tail, while others might be square or U-shaped when viewed as a cross section. A flat tail like this will move like a ribbon fluttering in the wind.*

*This dragon's coiling neck can spring its head forwards with terrific speed, much like a springing python. Note that the neck is segmentally armoured. Its thick, scaly sections protect it from attack.*

Experiment with some neck and tail shapes, using the examples opposite as a starting point. The neck often has a more complex muscle arrangement than the tail; however, it is usually covered by details that hide these muscles.

## Many uses

Remember that the neck and tail are useful for balance, protection and for describing mood.

Without its tail, the long-necked dragon is poorly balanced, so when drawing your dragon, you should consider how these two components can be equally matched. The dragon can use its tail as a deadly weapon, so tails are quite often covered in sharp, vicious ridges or have a club-like end. Necks too may be adorned with protective spikes or fins. Tails can also be used to show emotion. Just think of how a cat's tail moves and positions itself when it is angry, content or hunting.

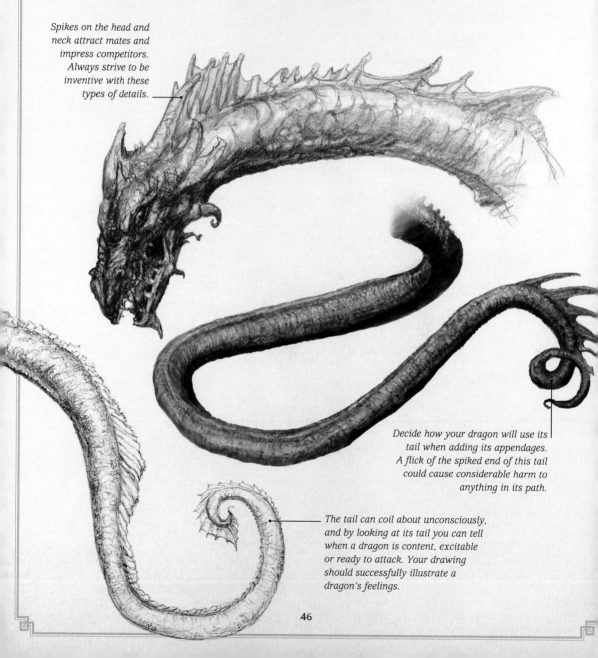

*Spikes on the head and neck attract mates and impress competitors. Always strive to be inventive with these types of details.*

*Decide how your dragon will use its tail when adding its appendages. A flick of the spiked end of this tail could cause considerable harm to anything in its path.*

*The tail can coil about unconsciously, and by looking at its tail you can tell when a dragon is content, excitable or ready to attack. Your drawing should successfully illustrate a dragon's feelings.*

Drawing the tail and neck gives you the opportunity to experiment with little details and ornamentation that you can use throughout the dragon. Almost anything goes in terms of horns, appendages and bumps on these body parts.

Use these two pages to draw different types of necks and tails.

# TALONS AND TEETH

The most foreboding part of the dragon is its terrible toothy smile. Next to that in evoking great fear are the dragon's powerful claws. One or the other can pierce and harm a human body in awful ways.

**Talon inspiration**
Although talons across the animal kingdom vary in their colourings and skin or scale coverings, all share similarities to the human hand in their formation.

*Fig. 1:* Emu foot
*Fig. 2:* Crocodile rear foot
*Fig. 3:* Eagle talons

**Teeth inspiration**
You can borrow a wealth of ideas from nature when you imagine your dragon's teeth. In addition to looking at size and shape, check the positioning, and look closely at textures and tones.

*Fig. 1:* Tiger
*Fig. 2:* Warthog
*Fig. 3:* Crocodile
*Fig. 4:* Viper

Look for your own examples of teeth and talons in the natural world, and attach or sketch them out here. Make a note of how you might adapt them for your dragon creations.

The dragon's claws can be a particular problem. Quite often dragons use their forelegs as arms and their claws as hands. If this is the case, you'll need to compromise on this structure to make it work in both cases. Women with unusually long fingernails are often unable to perform simple tasks required of the normal hand; therefore, an intelligent dragon with a library should not have excessively long claws.

## Hind and front legs

A dragon doesn't walk flat-footed but on its toes (much like someone wearing high-heeled shoes does), so it's important to keep this in mind when drawing a dragon's hind legs.

A good way to imagine a dragon's front paw is to look at and draw from your own hand. Adjust the proportions in your drawing so your hand no longer looks human, and greatly exaggerate every bump, stretch of skin and wrinkle on it.

*Imagine a dragon's hind leg as a human foot on tip toes, but with a claw on the heel.*

*Rather than flat toenails, a dragon's claws grow thickly upwards out of where the toenails are on a human foot, and then curve downwards.*

54

Have a go at drawing front and hind legs and feet. Add some scales
and talons to complete the look.

# Biting power

Look in the dragon's mouth and you may see huge fangs or small, menacing, razor-sharp canines. A good way to make a dragon even more menacing is to pull back its lips to expose the gums. It's perfectly fine to place the dragon's teeth on the outside of its mouth.

It's quite unusual to look into a dragon's mouth and see the teeth of a herbivore, no matter how peaceful that dragon is. However, your dragon doesn't have to have teeth at all to be a dragon; a deadly bite is all that matters.

*The larger a dragon's teeth are, the wider its mouth will have to open. Keep in mind that there are no rules for how wide a dragon can open its mouth. It can unhinge its jaw like a snake if need be.*

*You can't go wrong studying dinosaurs if you want to create some terrific dragon teeth. Like dinosaurs, a dragon would likely have new teeth growing in all the time. Note the smaller teeth growing in here.*

*Don't be surprised if your dragon looks like it's smiling. When you smile you bare your teeth, so it's quite similar to the threatening gesture of a snarling dragon.*

Copy the dragon mouths on the opposite page to practise putting the teeth in place.

**Teeth types**
A dragon is unlikely to have pearly whites, so stay away from making teeth with perfect surfaces. Draw them with all sorts of irregularities and cracks, and they'll seem all the more dangerous and realistic.

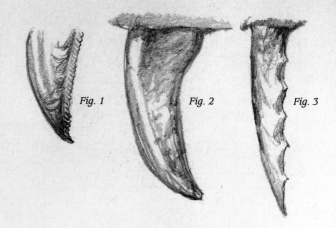

*Fig. 1*    *Fig. 2*    *Fig. 3*

Study these types of teeth and try them out on your own dragons.

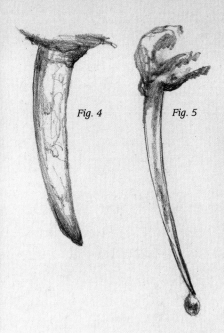

*Fig. 4*      *Fig. 5*

*Fig. 1* This type of serrated tooth is for grinding. No dragon would have humanlike molars, but this type of tooth works well for crunching up bone to get to the tasty marrow inside.

*Fig. 2* The curved tooth is used to grab and hold prey. It's sharp at the tip but somewhat roughly blunt or ridged at the back. If a jaw studded with teeth like these bites down on you, the only direction you'll be able to go is into the dragon's throat.

*Fig. 3* A razor-sharp serrated tooth is for grinding and cutting away flesh. We typically think of a dragon as a predator, but it can also be a scavenger. Such teeth are useful for tearing up a carcass.

*Fig. 4* A blunt, hard tooth like this is for puncturing prey. A dragon can bite and release its victims quickly, leaving them to bleed to death.

*Fig. 5* This is very much a fang rather than a tooth. Note the drop of venom on the tip. Expect fangs like this to be found on smaller dragons rather than large ones. Large dragons don't need poisonous fangs to make a kill.

Practise drawing dragon mouths from different angles, and decide how this affects which teeth can be seen.

# SKIN

No matter how sensitive-to-insult a dragon may be, it will be drawn with thick skin. Its skin can be smooth like a dolphin's, or it can have the tough hide of an elephant or the scales of a lizard.

**Inspiration from nature**
Look at the textures of the world around you. You can find some very dragon-like skin on animals, plants and trees. Nature is a great source of reference and is also free!

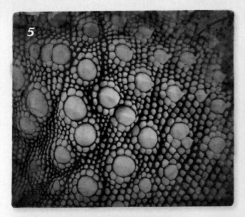

*Fig. 1:* Dried mud
*Fig. 2:* Dried leaf
*Fig. 3:* Snake scales
*Fig. 4:* Feathers
*Fig. 5:* Iguana skin
*Fig. 6:* Crocodile skin
*Fig. 7:* Fish scales
*Fig. 8:* Tree bark
*Fig. 9:* Lichen on rock

Collect your own textural examples here, making notes on why you are drawn
to them and how you might recreate them.

A nice thing about dragon skin is that it helps describe the animal's form. When you're drawing a mythical creature, it's sometimes necessary to give a few extra indications of the form. The natural skin texture of the dragon helps you do this.

## Choosing your skin

Are dragons mammals, reptiles or dinosaurs? They are what you want them to be, so you can give them any type of skin you want. It can look much like a dinosaur's skin or a reptile's. Many types of animals have scales on parts of their bodies, and they provide great reference for the creation of your own art. You could also study rhinoceroses and elephants at the zoo. A variety of horns and spines cover dragons, and you can have fun inventing your own kinds.

Keep in mind that there is a tonal and colour texture to a dragon, as well as a physical, tactile texture. Think of these as two layers of dragon skin. You'll also have to keep in mind highlights and shadows separately from texture.

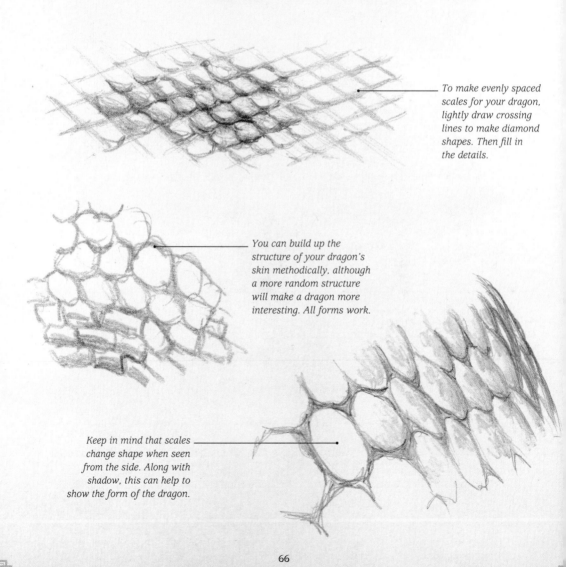

*To make evenly spaced scales for your dragon, lightly draw crossing lines to make diamond shapes. Then fill in the details.*

*You can build up the structure of your dragon's skin methodically, although a more random structure will make a dragon more interesting. All forms work.*

*Keep in mind that scales change shape when seen from the side. Along with shadow, this can help to show the form of the dragon.*

Try drawing random and ordered textures that could be used on your dragon drawings.

Now try applying your favourite skin effects to your own dragon bodies and limbs. How does the skin texture change in the different areas?

# ANATOMY AND PROPORTION

A study of the anatomy of the six-limbed dragon gives a good grounding in dragon art, and what you learn here can be translated to work with any type of dragon: remove the wings to make a flightless dragon; remove everything else but the spine to make a serpentine creature.

The six-limbed dragon is made up of a torso, four legs, a long neck and tail, and wings. The fun in making a dragon is that it is so ill-defined that you can play with the proportions of these elements to a great degree. However, the relationship and proportions of the elements with regards to each other still need to be considered carefully in order to create a plausible creature.

**The bare bones**
Understanding the basic anatomy of the dragon as a whole will help you to define your own dragon forms. This dragon has been stripped of its flesh and muscles and coloured so that you can clearly see the bones, wings, body shape and appendages.

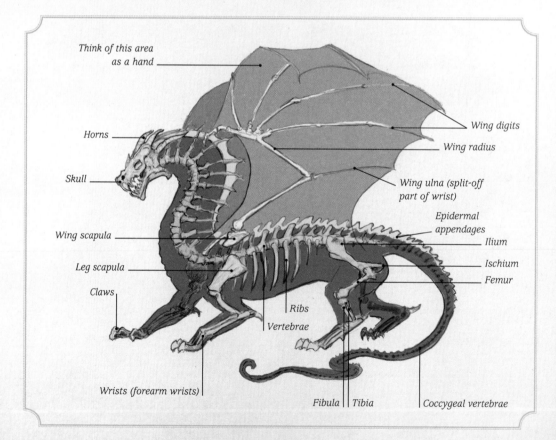

Think of this area as a hand

Horns

Skull

Wing scapula

Leg scapula

Claws

Wrists (forearm wrists)

Ribs

Vertebrae

Wing digits

Wing radius

Wing ulna (split-off part of wrist)

Epidermal appendages

Ilium

Ischium

Femur

Fibula

Tibia

Coccygeal vertebrae

Copy the diagram opposite, then try drawing it again but changing the proportions of some parts. What do you need to do to make sure the creature looks plausible all over?

# Using projection for proportion

Projection is a useful drawing technique and a nifty way to help you draw your dragon in proportion. By using corresponding lines to guide you, you can make sure your dragon stays the same proportionally from different angles and continues to look like the dragon it's supposed to be.

Consider projection as an exercise or a way to solve drawing problems, but it can also have a practical application. If you've designed a dragon character to be used in a cartoon, you're going to want to make sure that it stays the same throughout. Using a graphic like the one shown below is a useful tool to refer back to.

**Your dragon lineup**

Imagine you've posed your dragon on a pedestal, but once you've done one careful drawing of him, he then flies away. To make three more accurate drawings of him you'll need to use your imagination, but you can also use measurements from your first drawing.

*Make a profile drawing of your dragon on the left side of the page. Starting from the top of the drawing and moving down, take a ruler and carefully mark the important details. To the right, place a horizontally corresponding mark. This is the beginning of your 'dragon lineup'.*

*Draw horizontal lines across the page joining the marked important points. Draw the dragon from the back view, lining up the important parts so they are level with the corresponding points in the profile view. Note that from behind you can more easily see that the knees of the rear legs are angled outwards.*

*Use the same process to draw your dragon from a three-quarter view, referring closely to the previous two drawings. This view tends to tell you more about a subject. Note that from this view you can see that the wings and legs aren't on the same plane as their opposing parts, as they might seem in the profile.*

*An oval was used to recreate the same curve to the wings as seen from the back view. The front and back views could almost be mirror images of each other. You may find it useful to use ovals or other shapes to help you draw your dragon parts in proportion. Note that from this view the elbows of the front legs are angled outwards.*

Now make your own 'dragon lineup' and use the horizontal guidelines to judge proportion as you alter the view of your dragon.

Use the tips you have been given to draw different types of dragon and from different angles.

# DRAGON TYPES

There are six basic types or physical forms of dragons. Most are fictional. None of these categories makes sense in terms of scientific classification and none of the dragons are connected along any evolutionary path. These are discrete creatures, even though they are all dragons by name. Still, you need to know these basic forms and how they move if you are to draw them. Fortunately, it all follows somewhat logically.

# SERPENT OR WYRM

*(nullus-limbis serpentis)*

The serpent dragon is like a snake, eel or worm, with no arms, legs or wings and a lion-like or reptilian head. Despite its lack of wings, the serpent type can still achieve flight. This dragon can also be a sea serpent or sea dragon. There is a real fish called a sea dragon, but it is not the same thing.

## VITAL STATISTICS

**Habitats:**
Foggy lower lands, clouds and waterways: lakes, seas, oceans

**Personality:**
Sneaky, duplicitous, clandestine and ravenous

**Diet:**
Carnivorous, fond of warm-blooded animals, especially humans

**Size:**
Anywhere from snake-sized to the circumference of a planet

**Special characteristics:**
Tempts people to be immoral

Copy the serpent dragon opposite.

*Although they grow to fantastic sizes, a whale is no match for the terrible power possessed by this aquatic leviathan, the sea serpent.*

Fill these pages with your own serpent dragons.

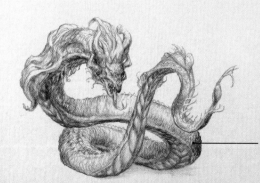

You won't find a more evil monster than this curled-up killer serpent. Its body is infused with a quick-acting poison. What it lacks in limbs is made up for in cunning.

# Winged Serpent

*(pennatus serpentine)*

A popular dragon form in literature, this is exactly like the serpent dragon, except that it has wings. The wings are typically attached near the head and the dragon can fly. This can also be a sea creature.

## Vital Statistics

**Habitats:**
Ancient gardens, dreams, nightmares and waterways

**Personality:**
Mischievous, angelic, deadly and mysterious

**Diet:**
Ghosts, fond of warm-blooded animals, fairies

**Size:**
Anywhere from snake-sized to the circumference of the moon

**Special characteristics:**
Can be ghost-like, ephemeral or magical

Copy the winged serpent dragon opposite.

Fill these pages with your own winged serpent dragons.

*This is the ephemeral form of the winged serpent. It's lovely in its movements but can become solid enough to strike a deadly blow with the hooked tips of its wings.*

# Pre-modern Fable

*(fore-bipedis pennatus serpenti)*

This is perhaps the strangest
dragon form. It is quite snake-
like, but with wings and
forearms though no rear
legs. In this form it can run
the range of reptilian to
mammalian characteristics.

## VITAL STATISTICS

**Habitats:**
Rocky lands, tunnels
and forests

**Personality:**
Clever, nasty, curious,
philosophical and ravenous

**Diet:**
Carnivorous, fond of warm-
blooded animals, especially
dwarves

**Size:**
Human- to polar-bear-sized

**Special characteristics:**
Does not observe physical
laws, magical

Copy the pre-modern fable dragon opposite.

Fill these pages with your own pre-modern fable dragons.

*This dragon flies as if it's lighter than air. As it twists through the sky it spots prey, swooping down and seizing it with its powerful forearms.*

# CONTEMPORARY MYTHICAL

## *(quadru-limbis pennatus draconi)*

This dragon is structured much like a bat, with two wings and two rear legs. The wings are used as arms as well as for flying. This type of dragon uses its thumbs for grabbing and holding objects or for walking. It rarely walks far on its hind legs. Birds are physically similar to this type of dragon, but birds use their feet for holding objects; not their wings, as bats do.

## VITAL STATISTICS

**Habitats:**
Rocky lands, mountains, caves

**Personality:**
Clever, friendly, deadly, sentient

**Diet:**
Carnivorous, fond of warm-blooded animals, especially human virgins

**Size:**
Bat- to skyscraper-sized

**Special characteristics:**
A keen fire-breather, hoards gold and jewels, keeps a library, can talk

Copy the contemporary mythical dragon opposite.

Fill these pages with your own contemporary mythical dragons.

*A four-limbed dragon is eloquent in the air but a bit awkward on land, so expect them to have limited movement on the ground. When drawn upright they'll hop or waddle instead of walking, spending most of their time perched on rocky outcroppings.*

# FLIGHTLESS DRAGON

*(quadrupedis draconic or varanus typis)*

This type of dragon comes in two forms, both of which move on four legs and can't fly. The mythological type moves like a dog, lion or horse. It looks much like a standard dragon and can gallop. The actual earthly dragon, the Komodo dragon, is a lizard and does not gallop, but waddles, moving the way a fish does through water, swinging its body horizontally with each step. If you want to give this lizard wings, you can. There are no hard and fast rules.

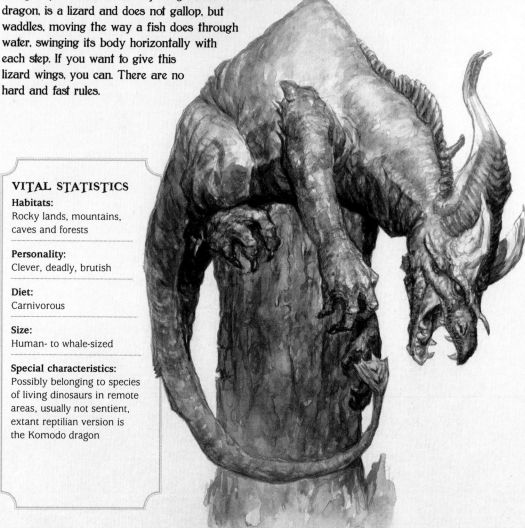

## VITAL STATISTICS

**Habitats:**
Rocky lands, mountains, caves and forests

**Personality:**
Clever, deadly, brutish

**Diet:**
Carnivorous

**Size:**
Human- to whale-sized

**Special characteristics:**
Possibly belonging to species of living dinosaurs in remote areas, usually not sentient, extant reptilian version is the Komodo dragon

**Copy the flightless dragon opposite.**

*This guy is a low walker. Even though it is a quadruped, it doesn't move like the dragon of legend but more like a lizard.*

Fill these pages with your own flightless dragons.

*The long and sinewy dragon is a popular non-winged dragon in many stories. Although it has legs, it moves more like a snake.*

# LEGENDARY CLASSIC

*(hexa-limbis pennatus draconis)*

To some, the six-limbed dragon is the true dragon form. It runs and walks on all fours, and its forearms can be arms as well as legs. It has huge wings to fly with and it can breathe fire. In mythology and literature, it comes in many different sizes. It is also the most difficult dragon to draw.

## VITAL STATISTICS

**Habitats:**
Mountains, caves, rocky landscapes, churches

**Personality:**
Intelligent, friendly, deadly, sentient

**Diet:**
Carnivore, fond of warm-blooded animals, especially human virgins

**Size:**
Bat- to skyscraper-sized

**Special characteristics:**
Fire-breathing, hoards gold and jewels, interest in literature, can be friendly to humans, can talk, makes a good pet if small

# Copy the six-limbed dragon opposite.

*The six-limbed dragon can be huge. Note how this one dwarfs the castle.*

Fill these pages with your own six-limbed dragons.

*This is a scavenger dragon similar to a vulture in its diet. Its large jaw is powerful enough to grind bones.*

# BRINGING YOUR DRAGON TO LIFE

In order to create fantasy art that appears realistic, you have to feel the life in the thing you are making up. You'll want to mentally have the dragon in the room with you, to sense its weight as the floorboards creak under it, touch its form and feel its texture. You need to be exposed to its full ferocity, intelligence or playfulness. The more you use your imagination, the better you'll become at seeing what's not truly there, an approach that is, by far, the best for bringing your dragon to life.

# LEARNING TO VISUALISE

To make your own unique dragons, you'll need to expand your ability to visualise. Completing the exercises described over the next few pages will help you to do just this. Repeat the exercises as regularly as possible for at least a year.

Although there are many theories regarding what makes humans different from other animals, it could be argued that our greater ability to visualise is what has given us an evolutionary edge over our ancient forebears. Other animals and early hominids have used tools, but what other animal makes representational art? Our ability to visualise is so great that we can make a picture of our visualisations by hand. This ability is not a lightweight one either. It is the start of every great human project: architecture, tool making, machines, bridges and boats to ocean liners all come when people visualise their plans.

The lessons that follow are designed to exercise the visual cortex in your brain and encourage it to grow larger, enabling you to see and draw more accurately.

## Observe and translate

Look for a man-made object of moderate complexity. It should be a solid object that you can easily see all the sides of, such as a toy, an ornament, a shoe, a kitchen appliance or a tool. Take your time and study the object carefully, moving it or walking around it.

Now close your eyes and try to visualise the object. What are its various shapes: squares, rectangles, ovals, or spheres? How is it proportioned? Open your eyes and study the object more closely. Then try again to visualise it with your eyes closed.

When you are satisfied that you're seeing the object well, put it out of sight, then draw it. A simple line drawing will do. Don't worry about tone. When your drawing is complete, return to your subject and compare it to the drawing. Notice where you may have forgotten something, or where an element may be slightly out of proportion. Find out what other people think of the drawing compared to the object.

Repeat this exercise several times over a period of days with different objects, and your observational skills will definitely improve.

Study your chosen object from all angles, then draw it without looking at it.
Continue to practise this technique with different objects.

# Draw living creatures

Drawing from life is essential practice, and working back and forth from imagining to drawing from life is a very quick way to learn.

Try visiting a zoo and drawing the animals there, or, if you have pets, watch how they move and draw them both from life and from your imagination. Turn to books and nature shows on television and the Internet, and pause on your subject in order to draw it. The better you understand animals, the better you'll be able to create a wide variety of dragons. The more you draw, the easier and quicker your visualising will become.

Practise drawing animals from life, then try drawing from your memories.

# Visualise in three dimensions

Here's another neat way to give your visual cortex some exercise. This is an advanced exercise, probably best attempted after you've learned some anatomy. You may want to start with simple objects first.

Find a figurine or sculpture of a person or animal. A sculpture is the ideal subject, something fairly realistic and fully three-dimensional, although a toy, plastic dinosaur, bust or doll of some kind will do if positioned interestingly.

Here's the tough part: you'll be drawing the sculpture not from the angle you're seeing it at, but from a view that is a one-quarter turn from where you are. When you have finished, compare what you drew to the actual view from that angle.

The point of this exercise is to get you to see and think in three dimensions. This is very important when you want to make a lifelike and believable dragon.

As a further test, draw or work from a drawing of a dragon from this book. Then imagine that you're alternately positioned like one of the four young dragon art students, pictured below.

**A different point of view**
If you look at the thought balloons above each of the dragons' heads, you'll see what they see from their particular angle. Note that none of the drawings represent how you see the dragon model yourself. All of the thought balloon drawings are at a lower eye level (the level of the dragon students) than yours and are from a different point on the circle.

Imagine you are viewing a three-dimensionl object from a different viewpoint, a quarter turn from your current view. Use this page to keep practising this exercise.

# STARTING POINTS FOR A DRAWING

The best way to approach a complex subject is to break it down into its component parts. Drawing a fully realised dragon requires knowledge of dragon anatomy, light, colour and texture. There are a number of ins, outs, twists and turns. To better understand how a dragon's body is structured, simplify its form into rectangles and then into more complex planes.

Use the following methods to better understand dragon form. If you can think of your dragon in terms of basic geometric shapes, it should help you project it into the third dimension, as well as give you the ability to draw it from a number of angles. It will also help you to understand how to shade your dragon.

## Put the dragon in a box

Take a quick gesture drawing that looks flat, and draw a rectangular box around it to get a better sense of the dimensions. Ultimately, this is a way of thinking that allows you to see form in a more concrete manner. Even though light, shadow and highlights are how you can show the shape of a dragon, these elements can just as easily confuse you when you're first understanding its structure.

*This dragon in profile can more easily be imagined in a three-quarter view if you see it inside a box. Even in profile, a dragon's head should have a sense of depth.*

*Here, the box is turned and you can see the dragon's face from a different angle. There's a little bit of three-point perspective in this turn. This helps give your dragon a greater sense of depth.*

Make quick dragon sketches and draw boxes around them to better understand the dimensions at play.

## Begin with boxes

Start by breaking the dragon up into basic rectangular shapes. Lightly draw the rectangles at the angle you want your dragon to be, and then begin to 'flesh out' the shapes. Once you've done this a few times, you'll find that you'll be able to imagine the third dimension without drawing the shapes at all.

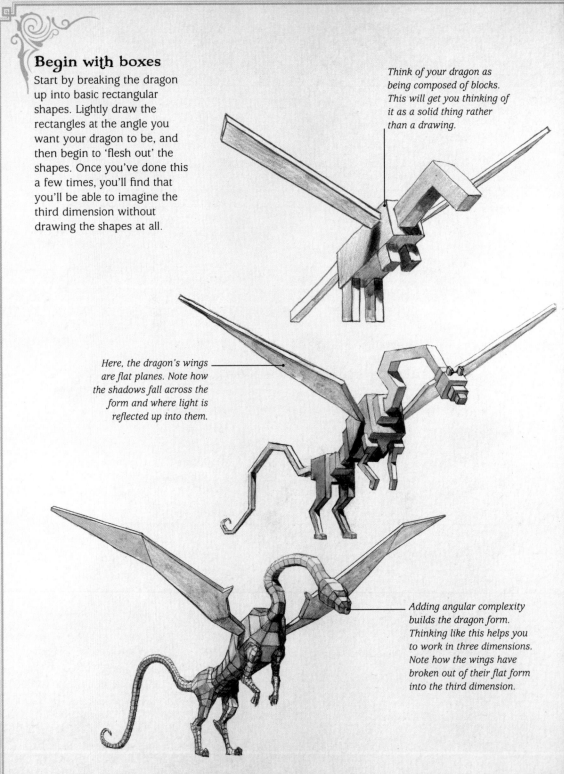

*Think of your dragon as being composed of blocks. This will get you thinking of it as a solid thing rather than a drawing.*

*Here, the dragon's wings are flat planes. Note how the shadows fall across the form and where light is reflected up into them.*

*Adding angular complexity builds the dragon form. Thinking like this helps you to work in three dimensions. Note how the wings have broken out of their flat form into the third dimension.*

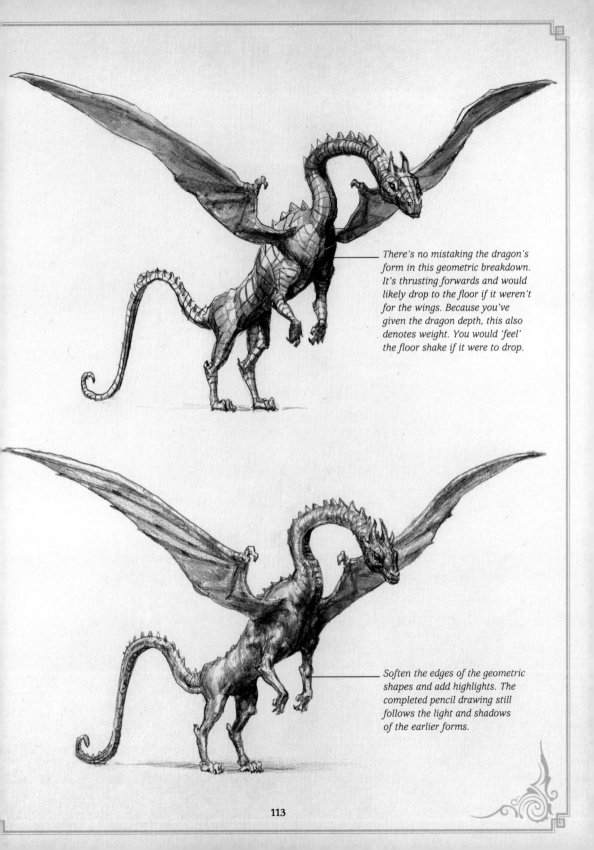

There's no mistaking the dragon's form in this geometric breakdown. It's thrusting forwards and would likely drop to the floor if it weren't for the wings. Because you've given the dragon depth, this also denotes weight. You would 'feel' the floor shake if it were to drop.

Soften the edges of the geometric shapes and add highlights. The completed pencil drawing still follows the light and shadows of the earlier forms.

Use these pages to draw your own dragon, starting with a basic 'skeleton' of rectangular shapes, as described on pages 112-113.

# DRAWING MOVEMENT AND GESTURE

Now that you can imagine your dragon's three-dimensional form, and visualise it from different angles, it's time to enter the fourth dimension... movement.

## Gesture drawings

Action tells the story of what is about to happen, what is happening or what has just happened. To illustrate the unfolding drama, you must feel the dragon's power and sense its path. Making a series of quick, action gesture drawings is a good way to accomplish this. Here are several examples. When you draw, you should think about the forces involved: Is your dragon a lightweight or a heavyweight?

The lower dragon's tail is curved just as it springs into the air, but it will straighten to help the dragon's forwards momentum. Note the differing wing and tail positions of the airborne dragon on top as it comes in to land.

Standing up is awkward for this type of dragon, which only does so to intimidate an attacker or see over an obstruction. Note how the neck curves back to help it balance.

This dragon advances on its hind legs and is ready to drop to all fours to run or spring into the air. Note that the right hind leg is drawn in two positions. It's fine to draw limbs in different positions over the same figure, to see what works best.

The best way to capture movement is by drawing quickly, so aim to spend just one to two minutes on each gesture drawing.

## Using action lines

Imagine a line running along your character's spine. A straight line suggests a stationary pose, whereas a curved line has a force and attitude that evokes movement. Look at photographs of people or animals in action and trace the line of action through their poses.

To feel the force of your dragon, you need to think about the way you move as a human. What position would you take if you were spitting out fire, making a quick turn as you run or leaping into the air? Imagine yourself as a dragon, and feel this as you draw.

Drawing dragons in action isn't an exact science but something you have to feel in the form of body movement. The sense of how your own body and other bodies move is called kinesthesia. If you can access that as you draw it will help you a great deal, but you'll still have to keep in mind how an animal that's different from you will move as well. Anthropomorphizing too much will keep you from creating a greater variety of dragons.

To give your action pieces more force, simplify your drawings into action lines, as shown below.

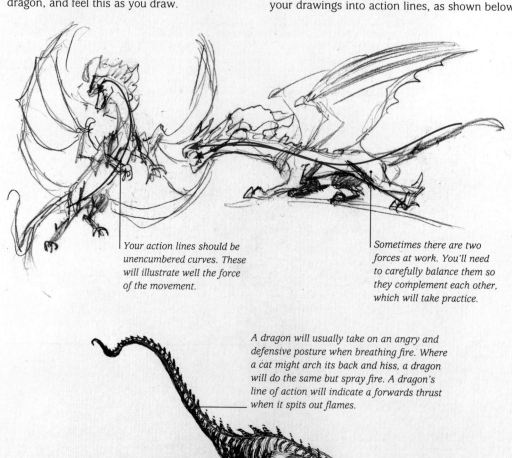

*Your action lines should be unencumbered curves. These will illustrate well the force of the movement.*

*Sometimes there are two forces at work. You'll need to carefully balance them so they complement each other, which will take practice.*

*A dragon will usually take on an angry and defensive posture when breathing fire. Where a cat might arch its back and hiss, a dragon will do the same but spray fire. A dragon's line of action will indicate a forwards thrust when it spits out flames.*

Draw a dragon in a movement pose, then draw in the dominant action line. Does it form a flowing curve, or do you need to adjust the creature's posture? Experiment with different positions and record what is effective and what doesn't work.

# Developing dragon form

Once you've got the action you want with quick gesture sketches, you can use them as a basis from which to draw a fully articulated and detailed dragon. Many artists print out their quick sketches at a larger size and trace over them to match movement closely, although you may prefer to redraw because something new and interesting might happen when you do so. When you have a nice action thumbnail, try drawing it again even smaller. By making it smaller you will probably eliminate the unnecessary lines that interrupt the action.

As you are developing your action drawing, it's important to remember that the more strenuous the dragon's movements are, the more its muscles will stand out. Tendons will pop between the muscles and the joints like tightly banded ropes. Also, the more a muscle is strained, the more angular it becomes. In a lean dragon even the muscle fibres will show. These are important considerations if you are working towards creating a realistic and lifelike dragon.

**Muscle placement**
Remove the lines you don't like from your drawing. Lightly draw in lines for muscle placement. As you draw, try not to give up any of the sense of movement. Details tend to hide movement and you should aim to keep as much as you can.

**Starting point**
Know the feeling you're going for. It can run the range from subtle to extreme and still come across in very few lines. Establish the dragon's movement with quick lines. Now is not the time to worry about a clean-looking picture.

**Blocking**
Movement will always take place through all three dimensions. Make a separate quick sketch that considers your dragon as a series of blocks (see page 112). Use this reference guide as you add your details, so your dragon doesn't become flat. This is also a good way to establish your light source and shadows, before adding them to the finished piece.

## Adding weight

Nothing gives a dragon weight and reality like heavy shadows. This is called chiaroscuro, and it works very well at making dragons both powerful-looking and dramatic. Taking the established shadows from the previous block sketch, lay them in as midtones and darken them when you feel confident in their placement. Now you can add your surface details.

Use these pages to practise the exercise from pages 120–121.

# Giving your dragon a personality

We humans anthropomorphise everything. Because we're so homocentric, we see ourselves in everything, from pets, trees and cars to the weather. Sometimes we even see our deities on burned toast. We're mightily self-centred creatures. The fact is that other animals are different from us and there's a lot we can learn from them, especially when it comes to dragons. Your dragons may certainly possess human qualities, but let's not forget the wide array of possibilities in the vast animal kingdom. At this juncture, toss out your human bones and gestural tendencies in favour of the greater variety offered by other species.

**Horse-like dragon**
If you want your dragon to stand proudly, study the stance of a horse and incorporate key aspects into your dragon's pose.

**Placid dragon**
For an easygoing, docile dragon, your mind, attuned to the animal kingdom, couldn't do much better than the relaxed demeanor of a toad.

Think about the personalities that some animals seem to project. What is it about them that suggests this character? Make sketches of the defining features and try to replicate them in dragon terms.

## Animal demeanor

Every creature has its own collection of demeanors, and you can capitalise on that when creating your dragons. You can make your dragon ferocious by thinking of lions when you draw it; or it can be a curled-up, lazy fellow comparable to a house cat. Alternatively, imagine a playful puppy and it can easily take on the quality of a happy-go-lucky young dragon. Let this type of thinking happen naturally rather than by looking at pictures of animals. You can always do that later as you refine your drawing.

*This puppy-like dragon is an eager fellow anticipating a treat.*

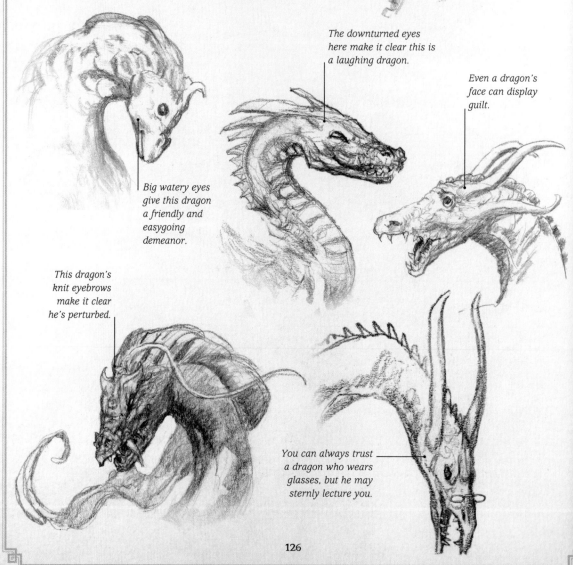

*The downturned eyes here make it clear this is a laughing dragon.*

*Even a dragon's face can display guilt.*

*Big watery eyes give this dragon a friendly and easygoing demeanor.*

*This dragon's knit eyebrows make it clear he's perturbed.*

*You can always trust a dragon who wears glasses, but he may sternly lecture you.*

Use this page to experiment with a range of dragon facial expressions.

# YOUR IMAGINATION TAKING FLIGHT

If you've ever flown a kite or felt an updraft under an umbrella, you have some sense of how dragon wings can provide lift. Along with forwards momentum, the basic principle will get your dragon off the ground.

Keeping all this in mind, imagine you're a dragon climbing into the clouds, raising and lowering your wings so that there's little resistance when you lift them up and forwards and greater resistance as you pull them down and behind you. As you reach your desired height, you'll move your wings less but still in a slightly circular motion. You can choose to circle riding updrafts like a kite, or if you have a great distance to travel you can maintain a regular wing beat. If you're in search of prey and spot it, you can pull your wings back and go into a steep but arcing dive. Unlike birds, you can choose between your front hands or back claws, or use all four to grab your lunch if it's particularly large. To come in for a landing you can use your wings like a parachute to land softly on your hind legs and drop to all fours. Now you've mastered dragon flight... in your imagination.

**Down**
When a dragon is flying at full force, it will pull its wings down, holding them in a position that grabs the most air until they almost touch below the chest. This dragon is pulling itself upwards and forwards with all its strength.

*Note how the wings come forwards when they're flapped. Imagine that your dragon is rotating them to pull itself through the air.*

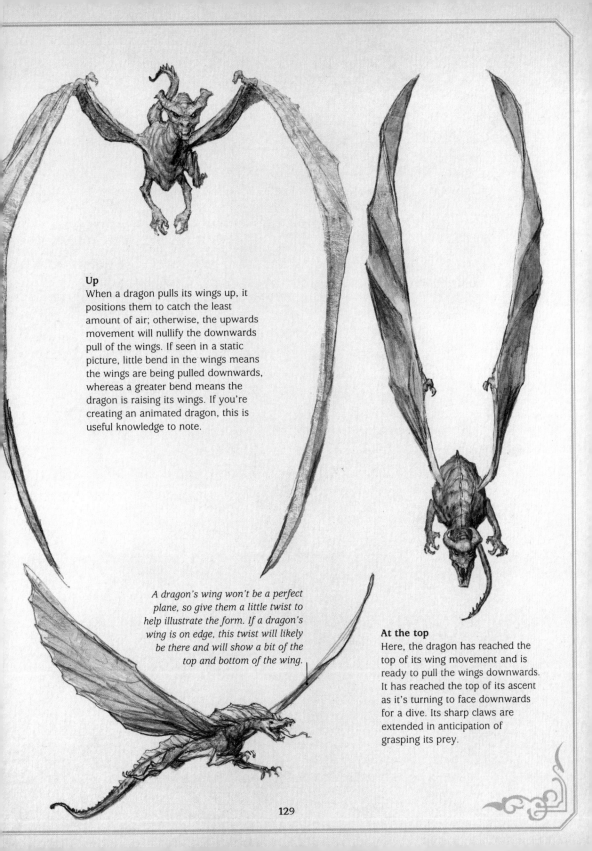

## Up

When a dragon pulls its wings up, it positions them to catch the least amount of air; otherwise, the upwards movement will nullify the downwards pull of the wings. If seen in a static picture, little bend in the wings means the wings are being pulled downwards, whereas a greater bend means the dragon is raising its wings. If you're creating an animated dragon, this is useful knowledge to note.

*A dragon's wing won't be a perfect plane, so give them a little twist to help illustrate the form. If a dragon's wing is on edge, this twist will likely be there and will show a bit of the top and bottom of the wing.*

## At the top

Here, the dragon has reached the top of its wing movement and is ready to pull the wings downwards. It has reached the top of its ascent as it's turning to face downwards for a dive. Its sharp claws are extended in anticipation of grasping its prey.

Practise drawing dragon wing positions by imagining the momentum and pressures against them during flight.

## Flight poses

Whether your dragon has just taken to the air, is mid-flight and soaring through the sky, circling in search of prey or diving down to catch it, you'll need a variety of poses at your disposal to suit your dragon's every need. Spend some time familiarising yourself with birds in flight (birds of prey are ideal), and take note of the shapes formed by their bodies at different stages of flight. Studying bird and bat wing mechanics and motions will help you understand how wings move, lift and thrust, and will allow your dragon to leap, glide, fly and dive convincingly.

### Steep dive

This is the start of a steep dive. Note how the dragon's legs seem to have just pushed off of something. When drawing a dragon in action like this, it's important to imagine that you're there: feel the wind, the sudden drop that you sense in your stomach, the strong torque of unexpected twists and the jarring power of sudden turns, and hear the sound of the dragon's giant flapping wings. This won't be a smooth ride.

### Wingspan

A dragon's wings must be big enough to lift it into the air. The larger the dragon, the wider the wingspan will have to be. Flight for a dragon is all about lift, and that means strong muscles, large wings and the ability to hold or move a lot of air. Notice how the finger bones of this dragon's wings all curve, to cup as much air as possible. The well-developed chest muscles are fully engaged, straining to pump the wings. Taut lower neck muscles pull the head back as the thighs are pulled into the body, compacting the form and allowing the wings to be as efficient as possible.

## Looking down

Because of the thinness of the dragon's skin membrane when it is stretched, you should be able to see the arms and digits beneath protruding through the skin in the same way that you can see the structure of a tent or umbrella. Typically from above, because the light comes from this direction, you'll see dragon wings in light and shadow rather than seeing through the wing. However, you can shift the colour here, the way one might see skin go white when it is stretched on a human knuckle.

## Aerial turns

Because a dragon is often a gangly six-limbed creature, you will need to show its body reacting more to aerial turns than you would a bird. Your typical bird's body is more compact. Imagine that, in mid-flight, this dragon sees something of great interest appear. To help it make a quick turn, it bends its arms backwards to reduce drag.

Now it's your turn to try out an array of flight poses.

# TEXTURE AND FORM

It's sometimes difficult to see the form in the texture of something. At other times it's difficult to see the texture inside the form. Sometimes there's form over form and texture over texture. All these elements can be confusing to the eye. However, you can train yourself to see all the aspects of a subject, despite how one may camouflage another.

Knowing that something is there doesn't mean that all of it has to make it into a drawing, but understanding what's there will help you to make a more convincing image. More so than with other genres of art, fantasy and science-fiction art deals with unfamiliar scenes and creatures. An artist working from life might not need to understand texture as well as a fantasy artist because his or her subject is there for careful examination. As fantasy artists we're making something up, and so it will serve us to delve deeper into texture than other artists, through a number of layers. The images here show a way of thinking rather than a true technique for making a picture. Here, you can see physical texture (the bumps and valleys), tonal variegation of texture (the colouration of the skin) and form (represented by light and shadow). The point of these illustrations is to show you how to think about a texturally complicated subject before you draw it. Keep these separate layers in mind as you work, and work them together for a fully formed dragon.

**Tactile texture**
Your eyes can't always see what your hands can feel, but knowing what a surface might feel like will help you to draw it. Some surfaces only show up within the highlights. This line drawing is an illustration of only the tactile texture of a dragon. The lines represent the 'ins', 'outs' and edges of the surface. In the real world this would be represented only by light, shadow and highlight on a surface.

**Shading over texture**
This illustration gives a sense of the shading that will go over the tactile and visual texture. Even though you will most likely be approaching these layers at the same time, it's good to understand these aspects on their own.

**Perfect skin**
This is what a dragon lit in normal light would look like if it had entirely nonvariegated skin, that is, skin of all one colour and shade. Only the eyes, the teeth and the comb have a different tone to them. It looks a bit too perfect, but you can clearly make out all the ins and outs without the confusing extra layer of tonal texture.

**One level only**
To get a sense of all the texture
involved, use the side of the pencil
to create random rough lines.
Draw the scales in more carefully,
though, and add darker spots over
lighter lines in the deepest crevices
of the dragon's skin.

**Everything combined**
Blotches, wrinkles and
discolourations have been added.
Now you can see some variation
in the tonal quality of the lines
representing tactile texture, and
that the tonal quality of the picture
is clearly influenced by light.
Highlights have brightened the
peaks of the dragon's skin, and
the shadows have soft edges.

Replicate the examples on pages 136-137 with your own dragon drawings, separating the layers of tactile texture (what you would feel if you touched the dragon), tonal texture (skin shading) and form (how the dragon is shaped by light and shadow).

# LIGHT AND SHADOW

Without lights and darks, without values, your drawing will look flat. It's only through light and shadow that the three-dimensional form is revealed. Living in such dark places as caves, deep seas and thick forests, dragons can cast some very big shadows.

Colour, texture, warms and cools add depth and dimension to your dragon art, but only if your lights and darks establish a good, solid foundation. Light reveals and sculpts the form. Think of your pencil as a torch moving over the dragon, revealing some areas clearly, some

indistinctly and others not at all. As you work, remember that the light and shadow 'shapes' must describe your dragon – the form of the wings, the curve of the neck and belly, the musculature of the limbs. Try stepping back and squinting at your work. This lets you see the values and big shapes, and gauge how they are working together. If in doubt, simplify. Three values (a light, middle and dark) are enough to describe the form well, and if you can't make something work with three values, the problem is not the lack of value range but rather that you are not using them to effectively define your dragon's shapes.

### Drawing light and shade
It can be difficult to tell why an area of something you're drawing from life is darker or lighter. Sometimes it's because less light is on the area; sometimes it's simply a darker area; perhaps it's a shiny area angled towards you, reflecting the light source back at you, or it's angled away from you and reflecting a dark area. By drawing from life regularly, you'll develop an instinct for this and be able to make your dragons more believable.

*You can't add highlights to a pencil drawing, so you have to know where they will appear and take note to not draw in those areas. It's best not to go too dark at the beginning stage of a drawing.*

*Your dragon will have varying tones in its shadows because there is almost always some ambient light bouncing into the shadowed areas. Certain areas, such as the underside of the dragon, pick up less ambient light and are therefore darker.*

## Cast shadow

When drawing your dragon you want to know where the light is coming from as well as how the shadow will be cast, so that you'll know what's lit by direct light and what's not. In a basic way, the dragon's silhouette can be laid down flat and looked at on edge to get a sense of its cast shadow in perspective. Typically, a shadow doesn't have to be perfect to be convincing. Any disturbance or wave to the ground will distort a shadow.

*Looking at the dragon's silhouette is a good way to study the creature's contours. By knowing a dragon's contours you can more easily project a shadow.*

*The sun has moved lower on the horizon to cast a slightly lighter shadow.*

## Low light

The dragon is turned clockwise from the profile view while maintaining the same pose, and the sun has moved lower on the horizon to cast a slightly lighter shadow. Looking down on the subject again, the dragon almost casts a perfect silhouette of its profile.

*The shadow darkens as the dragon's belly comes closer to the ground.*

*If separated, you wouldn't recognise this shadow as belonging to this dragon.*

## Ambient light

The dragon is standing in profile, with the light coming from above and a little to the left, distorting its shadow. Note that the shadow darkens as the dragon's belly comes closer to the ground, due to ambient or diffused light. Ambient light is your constant second light source. Hold a solid object over the ground on a sunny day, and notice how its shadow darkens as you move it closer to the ground.

## Lit from above

Here the viewer is looking down on the dragon, which is lit mostly from overhead and a little to the left. Its shadow doesn't show much of its form at all. Your eyes quickly adjust to the shaded part of the dragon, and you can see details in it despite most of its body being in shadow.

Draw your own dragons with the light source coming from different places, making a note of how this affects the shading on the dragon's body, and how it changes its cast shadow.

# DRAGON TEMPLATES

On the following pages is a collection of flat drawings of dragons, organised into the dragon types identified on pages 76–101. Use them to experiment with different concepts and overall approaches, or use them as a training tool to play with lighting, focus or points of interest, to help you define the characteristics of the dragon and the image that you want.

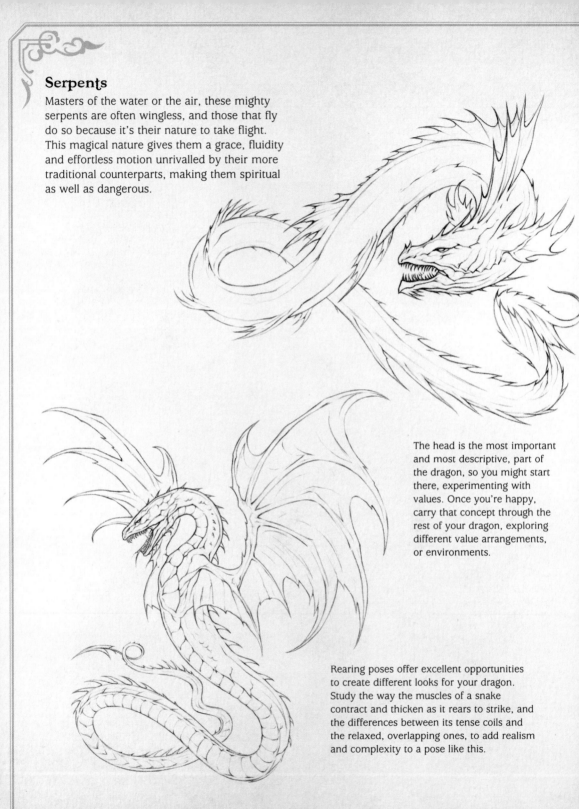

## Serpents

Masters of the water or the air, these mighty
serpents are often wingless, and those that fly
do so because it's their nature to take flight.
This magical nature gives them a grace, fluidity
and effortless motion unrivalled by their more
traditional counterparts, making them spiritual
as well as dangerous.

The head is the most important
and most descriptive, part of
the dragon, so you might start
there, experimenting with
values. Once you're happy,
carry that concept through the
rest of your dragon, exploring
different value arrangements,
or environments.

Rearing poses offer excellent opportunities
to create different looks for your dragon.
Study the way the muscles of a snake
contract and thicken as it rears to strike, and
the differences between its tense coils and
the relaxed, overlapping ones, to add realism
and complexity to a pose like this.

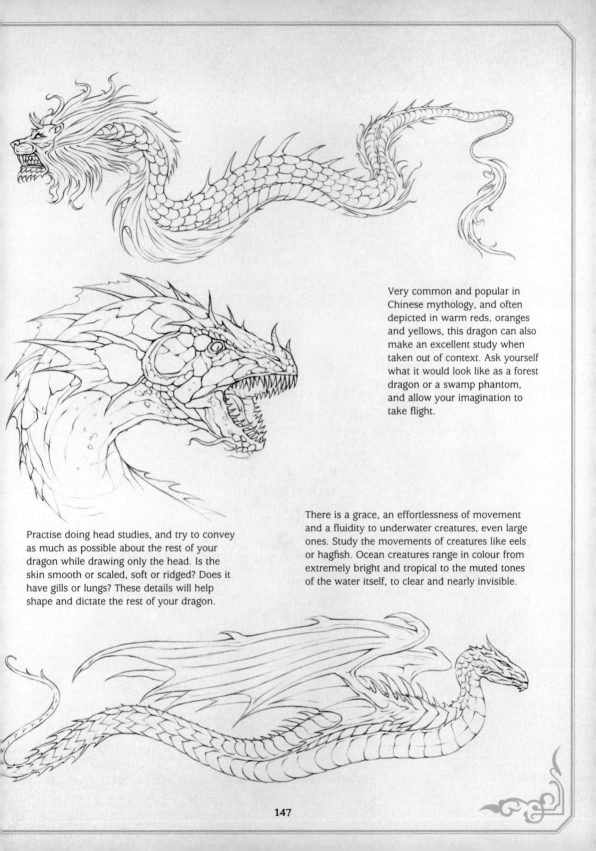

Very common and popular in Chinese mythology, and often depicted in warm reds, oranges and yellows, this dragon can also make an excellent study when taken out of context. Ask yourself what it would look like as a forest dragon or a swamp phantom, and allow your imagination to take flight.

Practise doing head studies, and try to convey as much as possible about the rest of your dragon while drawing only the head. Is the skin smooth or scaled, soft or ridged? Does it have gills or lungs? These details will help shape and dictate the rest of your dragon.

There is a grace, an effortlessness of movement and a fluidity to underwater creatures, even large ones. Study the movements of creatures like eels or hagfish. Ocean creatures range in colour from extremely bright and tropical to the muted tones of the water itself, to clear and nearly invisible.

## Pre-modern fable

These creatures are from a time when dragons were magical, mystical and more of a force of nature than anything malevolent or sentient. The long serpentine form, small wings and traditional reptilian head suggest a dragon more symbolic than anatomically accurate, a distinction that leads naturally to the development of certain types of dragons.

In spite of the very low viewpoint, the twists, turns and curves of this dragon provide a lot of depth and action. What shadow shapes, colours or lighting key would best capture the tense, coiled energy present here?

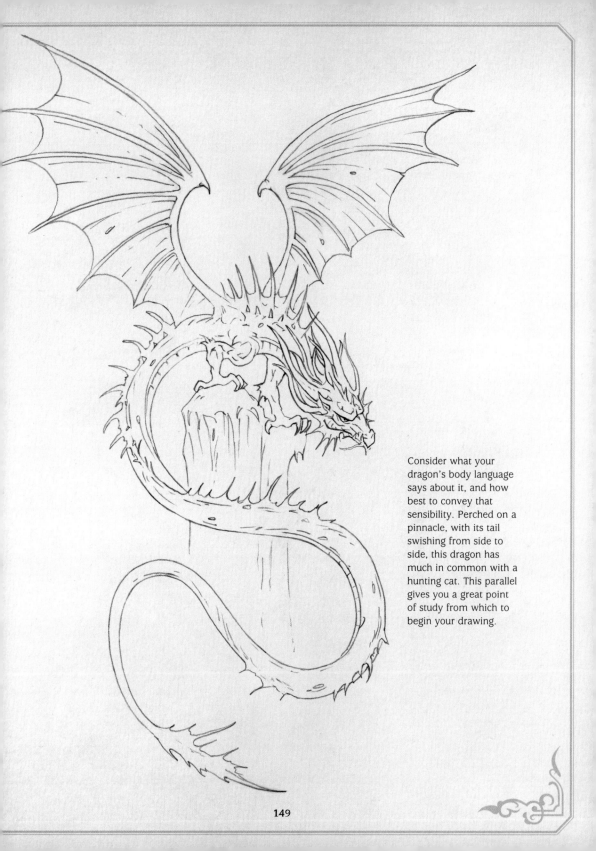

Consider what your dragon's body language says about it, and how best to convey that sensibility. Perched on a pinnacle, with its tail swishing from side to side, this dragon has much in common with a hunting cat. This parallel gives you a great point of study from which to begin your drawing.

Fantastical designs like this offer excellent
opportunities for nontraditional solutions.
This dragon could be made of air, light
or clouds – its design and movement less
governed by gravity and more by magic.
Ask yourself how a cloud dragon would
move, feed and think to get an idea of
what to emphasise or remove from the
drawing to best capture your concepts.

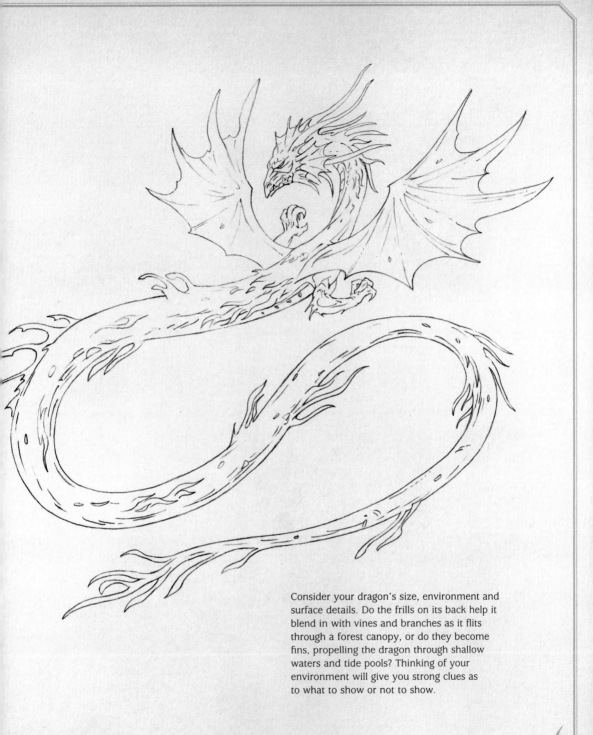

Consider your dragon's size, environment and surface details. Do the frills on its back help it blend in with vines and branches as it flits through a forest canopy, or do they become fins, propelling the dragon through shallow waters and tide pools? Thinking of your environment will give you strong clues as to what to show or not to show.

## Contemporary mythical

Elongated arms, massive wings and chest muscles
and a love of high, rocky places are the primary
characteristics of these dragons. The study of bats,
both walking and flying, is vital to drawing their
much larger cousins. Strive to balance the size
of these dragons against their speed and agility,
and look for ways to help convey motion, whether
it be through softened edges, depth of field,
use of lighting or the direction of your pencil
marks (marks that sculpt around the form
indicate volume; those that follow the
length of a form show motion).

Note how the 's' curve of the body and
tail indicate one direction, while the
wings prepare to drive the dragon forwards
in a new direction. What shadow shapes
and light placement would best describe
this? Ask yourself what you want to
emphasise – the dragon's current
movement, or its more imminent one?

The twisting and turning agility of this dragon is amazing, and explosively fast – characteristics to be emphasised in your drawing, every bit as much as the wonderful details of the head. With such a strongly foreshortened pose, the accurate use of shadow shapes is crucial for conveying the form clearly.

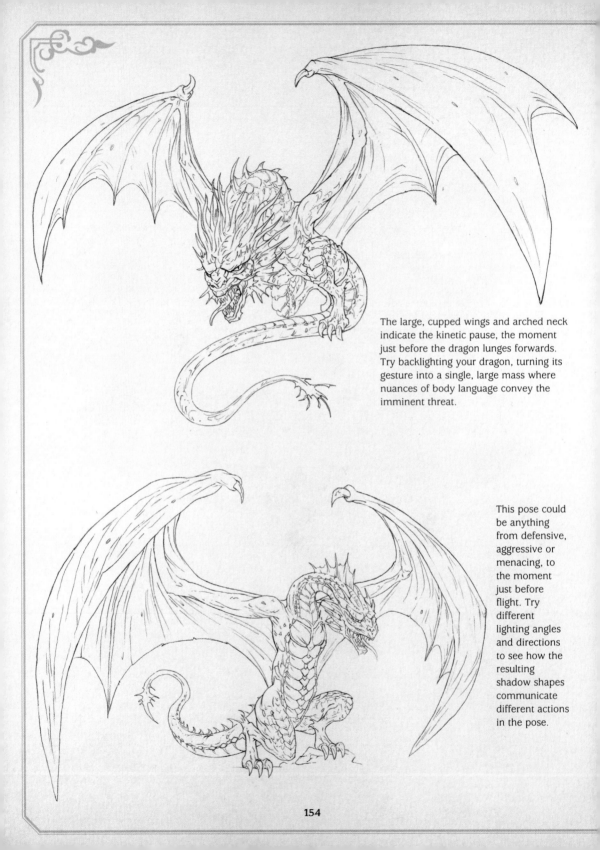

The large, cupped wings and arched neck indicate the kinetic pause, the moment just before the dragon lunges forwards. Try backlighting your dragon, turning its gesture into a single, large mass where nuances of body language convey the imminent threat.

This pose could be anything from defensive, aggressive or menacing, to the moment just before flight. Try different lighting angles and directions to see how the resulting shadow shapes communicate different actions in the pose.

# Flightless dragon

Large and dangerous, at times lithe and quick, at other times slow and brutish, these hunters of the ground, water, trees and rocks are still formidable foes. Based more closely on natural animals than most other dragons, these creatures represent a primal and direct threat; they thrive and survive on stealth, cunning or sheer strength and power.

With its long limbs, powerful tail and a suggestion of fins, this dragon may be at home in forests or near rivers and lakes. Emphasise the fins and downplay the scale textures for the smooth skin of a water dweller, or play with skin colouration and camouflage to create a forest dragon.

Long and lean, with well-defined muscles, this dragon has all the characteristics of a lethal predator. To further convey this nature, pay close attention to the eyes, the attitude of the head and the body language. Try lighting it from the front, to focus on the eye ridges.

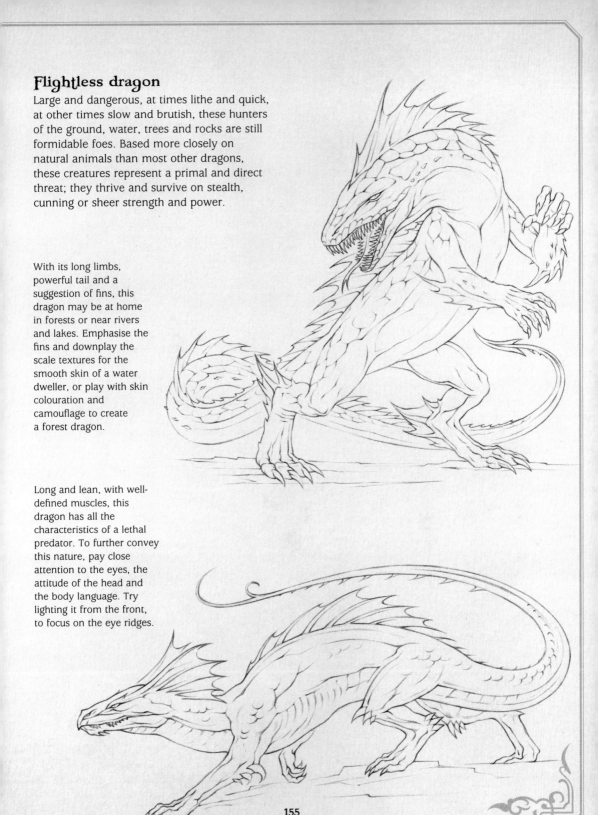

A desert dragon like this might take the colour and texture of sand and rock. How would its nature differ from a dragon that was brightly coloured? Where would you place your shadows, or what value key would you use to best convey the nearly invisible dragon of the sands?

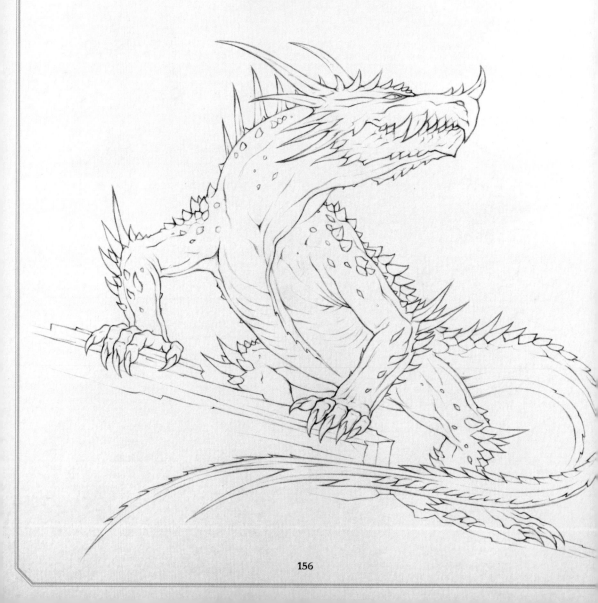

This dragon is a mass of spikes and scales, and like the modern-day lizard, you have to ask yourself why? What environment or conditions would give rise to such a formidable arsenal, and what aspects of that do you wish to focus on in your artwork? With so much detail, and so many small shapes, your shadows must be selectively and effectively edited in order to convey the overall shapes clearly.

## Legendary classic

These are the true mythological dragons, intelligent and fearsome. Combining traits of lions, lizards, dinosaurs and bats, they become something greater than the sum of their parts. Let your imagination reign when approaching these classics, and let your inner eye guide the design, staying true to the spirit, rather than any specific reference.

As comfortable and as formidable on the ground as in the air, your dragon should pose a threat, even when standing still. Study large predators in nature, and strive to capture the grace and power of these mighty hunters in your own dragons.

Start with a strong, clear concept, and be sure all your design choices support it. This dragon is turning, its back arched in attack. Try choosing your values to emphasise motion, aggression and attack, rather than anatomy, and consider what will most clearly convey these aspects of your dragon.

# CREDITS

The material in this book originally appeared in Tom Kidd's
*How to Draw and Paint Dragons*.

We would like to thank Dimitar Nikolov and Jan Patrik Krasny
for their contribution to the Dragon Templates
(pages 146–159).

While every effort has been made to credit contributors,
Quarto would like to apologise should there have been any
omissions or errors, and would be pleased to make the
appropriate correction for future editions of the book.

If you enjoyed this book, then check out
*Fantastic Creatures and How to Draw Them*,
published by Search Press (2018)